T0151074

ENTHUSIASM

ENTHUSIASM
Odes & Otium

Jean Day

ADVENTURES IN POETRY

Cover: Detail from an untitled painting on salvaged plywood by
the anonymous collective SNIFF, whose work can be viewed at
the Albany Waterfront Park (the "Albany Bulb"), a spit of landfill
on the east shore of the San Francisco Bay, just north of Berkeley.
Photo Fall 2005 by the author.

Book design by *typeslowly*
Printed in Michigan by Cushing-Malloy, Inc.

Adventures in Poetry titles are distributed to the trade through
Zephyr Press by Consortium Book Sales and Distribution
[www.cbsd.com] *&* SPD [www.spdbooks.org]

Library of Congress Cataloging-in-Publication Data

Day, Jean, 1954-
  Enthusiasm : odes & otium / Jean Day.
     p. cm.
  ISBN 0-9761612-3-0 (alk. paper)
  I. Title.

  PS3554.A9638E58 2006
  811'.54--dc22

9 8 7 6 5 4 3 2 FIRST PRINTING IN 2006

Adventures in Poetry
New York ● Boston
www.adventuresinpoetry.com

ACKNOWLEDGMENTS:

I am grateful to all who contributed to the completion of this book: to the George A. and Eliza Gardner Howard Foundation and the National Endowment for the Arts for generous financial assistance; to the MacDowell Colony, Peterborough, New Hampshire, for a place to work without distraction; and to the Redwood Library and Athenaeum, Newport, Rhode Island, where several of these poems took shape. Versions of some of them have appeared in *The Best American Poetry 2004*, *Crayon*, *Raddle Moon*, *Aufgabe*, *The Germ*, *Tongue to Boot*, *Electronic Poetry Review*, *26*, *Xanthippe*, *Sal Mimeo*, *Insurance*, and the *New Review of Literature*, whose editors I also heartily thank. Finally, thanks to Bula Maddison and Paul Harrill for the loan of hardware at two crucial moments.

I am living fast, to see the Time.

—Swift, *Tale of a Tub*

TABLE OF CONTENTS

UNDERSTORY

The mania for explanation   finds me   with you again   in Dudeville
buried in our dresses   Well, half   and half extended   sunward   The
rest works   out a deal below   a mother cloud afloat   in muddy folio
a type of so   much more   than this   twist   soaked in photo-
synthesis   beginning   every time the same   damn rain   drops dead
etceteras   sky bright in   patches   tufted   irrelevant and swell
among leaves   whose utility is   flak   hatched in the   wide (impolitic)
applied   rolling in rustic   not to say sea   not to be   shining
waves:

Odes

REASON

Our sensible subjects

    Men are mortal if Paris is in Texas
    Where stuff on boots is steeper than you
    Think along a bulky bank of sheer
      Sunrise an eponymous drink
        Customer Delight I think.
    Speak, Miantonomo; don't be so obsessed
        (Eponymous father of a hill)
    With bumper crops of retro cash
    The grass will grow
      Without us
        The ear might clear (or better yet
                        Unfold)
        In the Magnetic Bug Theater.

Where radio evolves into noise

    Got up, felt dubious.

    O happiness, death, and its reminder
    What passions speak for both of us out-of-
        Towners always
    Arterial people around a central clamp
      Or staple?
    Much country has been mapped in a vain
      Thicket but
        I go straight to the sun instead to bask
In the truth of the matter
Sucked from a slight tilt felt for example
      In Manhattan
      Canyons obsessed with right but not

Revision. Later Punjabi lunch.
    Bought a candle and read *Great Expectations*.

In which, trial by experiment

We lived solely off acorns, true?

Then how could our thoughts so dilapidate
    Our otherwise gorgeous tongues? Speech
        Flutters in loop dusk a dipper
            Slipping
Always farther upstream
            That's swell
    You who wonder
            Wandering analgesiacs
        Your pastry is waiting high to be eaten
        With just a knife and fork
    From which sweet dust flies
    On a wing and a reservation.
What's left to say on wooden lips can't float away
        Out of a paper bag
        It is said
Illuminations occur more outside
The skin (its projection) than in its little
    Vessels; take the logical utensil
        To rescue a nutshell in a frame
            Of oceanic lift
                Itself adrift as far as it goes
                    But suppose
The smudge pot in the arras lights
Just a sandy little pond
    A family swims in?

Whose decomposition

Obviously we are not the queen of France
And you are not in heaven
Jones may be guilty but she isn't bald

6

Smith then is innocent and Robinson lied
These were our true relations
Without double or doubt
Only the names have been changed
And if the lake drains northward
Into the Dripsweet Campaign?
Then Jones can sell her car
To the hill people and disappear
Without remainder
All the world loves a loner
If the pretty little girls
Prove recalcitrant the port itself
Will remain under junta control
Unless a remand comes
From the Colonial Office
Then the jig is up
Hawkshaw surely will have seen us
Going down to the river
And away

After taxes

The labor of the bee takes us straight to the money.
And the reason for this liquid?
  Equally, we face the same odds
      Melt in the canals
      Of our mothers' arms.
The candle remembers the economic
Quantity in a (European) night
      When even the curtains burned
                    Happiness.
Above Alexei Parschikov
  Lazy blimps broadcast
      dreamy ids awake
Mistaken everywhere for liberation.

Sun
   At midnight could have killed us
      Or I could teach them how to flip
The switch
         But why? A trace remains
    Breaking over chains

How high the error is
  Pregnant again by who knows
    Who
    Or what beyond the walking dunes
A paycheck floats unsuppressed
  In a letter on a droplet to a corporal
     Setting out
    Among lovable obstacles

PROSE OF THE WORLD ORDER

This blue
is nothing but elastic
sound everlasting a relapse
improbable neither vegetable
nor animal
not even personal but
sonorous as lexical hash
hypothetically
a novella by a fellow guest here
left finally dead
as matter might
stick to a wall
virgin in shape or exquisitely
scrawled
the gist of which is
We exist in places
otherwise strange and probably
impassible.
Yet here
yours is not the first face
to appear
surrounded upright
on two feet awake
stunned from the sleep of a Nobody

Curiously peering
into an icon of yourself
captive in a cubicle
(nice spot to adapt to
maybe
after channeling Emerson).
Some of us lack the luxury
of being nowhere

unaccountable
hence our methodism
(divine or boredom?)
and our jobs.
Scrip floats up for grabs
spun from thin air
for us gilded free
from the company
flywheels
of a motorized chair
slow boat from here
to there long since
locked away like a young
onion in the silt
shade of deferred and elegant
oaks standing
standing still standing
radiant
as dialectical ballast
to this alchemical
mixing of apparent opposites
gold and gas
first and last ecstaticle
motivating hillwise
as we ply broad day
light I say
its instants under plain
square sky
unreconstructed and leaving
behind us
in our exodus
our old Gestetner
booming
iambic as a house
gusseted to plackets in the hard

slippage
we'll always be known by
into the new

Solitude of a motor park.
Blue days equal almost salty
ones in the perpetuity of sight
seeing
whose sphincter clings
to a fleck overcome
with personality fluttering
naively perfect through sleep
where dialectical ballast is
the picture itself
and the prose of its obverse or
curses foiled when shove
comes to push
the mud of the flood
up to a door
like a hatch in the present
of absent disarticulation
strewn with little joints
of party mix; it's how we get
along (self-
selection) gently letting neighbors
know you're one of those
animals
endowed with speech *or* one of those who
listens. Plaid-suited
between the glorious lines
of the seven species of talk
(horizontal, uniform, and swimming)
my eyes have seen the coming
of our internal works by day
dropping the pretense when night

falls on all
six of us who call ourselves "I"
without abandon

And for how long?
You may be a cousin
twice removed from town
down alone in Shadow Valley
or so your tag suggests
just as someone else begins to whistle
Jenny Can't Sit Still
then commences
hanging out Old Warbler's rags
on sticks. The pastoral *it*
(yesterday's abjection
in today's machine)
was being reamed
by a contraption; all I know
is what the words know and the long
sonata for Nobody and
her ingot of a blue
tongue
(inexplicably thick
it seemed the spine of someone
else inside her
more metal than meter
meter than memory
and ticked).
Would she have anywhere to go but west
to east
to some unspeakably hackneyed
medical destination a depot
a desk from which
to contemplate the original definition of *sunset*
as financially secure?

The plaid animal thought not
furiously cribbing from notes
but willing then
to reset the counter at zero again
late as it was and ruined
with finger trouble. A claim
a double dose a middle a hose
make themselves friendly
to any living that wants to go
in (—fate
of any figure
in a picture). But what is
inside her except another brave scene
another burnt-out
antechamber—longer
paler … ? The plosive stream
smoothes out again
corrupted only by the failure
of dull correctives. Remember
Nobody's tongue?
When it shows up wet
will you stand flat?
Bother to call it Mother?
Rear up like a horse
to the original slap
of retraction? The sound
of which (appeal
wail—at last
a form of speech)
brings all the gold of the sky to bear
as particles of time
massed along the border
lane in nothing
fine
but a fly in the ardor of precision

ODE IN PENCIL

... *feet*, born first
into the west of a world
before its triangulation ...
            Which is where
the parents of the originals
(the *first* ones) sign
on to an underworld
downstairs (the jeep
follows along behind).
It's the taste of the sun
swollen on their tongues
that makes them spit,
"Whatever it is,
it's alive!" Socks
they arrive; stranger
they depart
            Last brief rays
in repetion's machine
set the scene [or *Spiel*]
on permanent sputter:
a woman entering
the frame of a murderous
cloud clobbers a man
ratcheting back
behind silent
credits (all clear
in underwear),
hogtied at the end
to the twang
of a player piano,
the small
unhappy voice of allegory
in snowy scrub the blood

ponders longer than seconds
and spreading
out from its unrecoiled arrest
so you may see days raging,
as days rage
          Scratched out.
Who should elaborate
while we stand up
in our hats? Feet flat
and on our way
from Necropolis?
I woke up singing your alien song,
little bird, the pirate chant
you mouth without
a hint of meaning (*hidey-ho*),
memorialized in an all-night
session leaving
nothing but a pencil.
"Farewell young stub,"
the tree might say, over-
determined off the face
of the map. "I saw you
people trying hard to win
friends
but I won't bend down
until the world reverses
its own subatomic
overflow"
          In a fictional
direction, delible
they set out: feet, parents,
stranger, sexed person,
pirate, tree, and me
into a material nightmare
(giant rusted spools, conduit

connecting what
to what, has-been mountains
looming over). Each tiny
idiolect as though
departing speaks
beyond the statue of its former
self, as though deforming
commemoration, the way "a stone
is nothing but weather"
and a stopping place
          Is an image
of thought. The (forbidden) easy
street noise turned to alleys
sullen with crows and the shape of feet
to come once detritus
stopped felling the nodding heads
of folks; it was what
they wanted to hear:
that an individual pivots
on a shortcut—the ear of the face
facing up
          Star on star,
which for him
(and his figure) became
melody, what birds
don't remember along
the road out of the song
with no particular protection
from the sun,
knees plainly pointing:
"Go here." The umpire
is fulfilling ancient orders
in the communal kitchen
for the little people who
won't decline more *mbs*

of RAM; a neck problem
prevents them
from looking up
into [uncorroboratable]
boundlessness
for an explanation
   I gave up milk
(a throbbing cataract with—
upsettingly—
no discernible bottom)
for less metrical feet
in the new economy
in the white dust
of the pencil factory
where they've switched
instead to shoes so we'll
have somewhere to go
to
washed, lost, and implied
in our own destinationless
sense of series
    After a stop
at Woolworth's for
supplies we reconnoiter
at the horizon, itself fortified
with flags and last
hats, a poignant
remainder of its own tendency
to disappear. I,
involuntary's volunteer
in a figure of radiant
blood
scribble up a slope
hand by foot
(and that dissolved

in a mouth)
buttressing the intention to
break in half
the *last* last lines
small and large and
instantly convertible
into firsts

WHAT THE SAWHORSE SAW

So the little sawhorse continued on her junket
Across a brierpatch into a firebucket
Pursued by a chainsaw knee-high to a matchstick
Monster for whom there are no less than twelve gates
All reversible … Hallelujah!

Was it music mercury
or milk that scratched
our bubbling innocent
half in half
swung low as the
time of your
life split out
by other means?
Sap ran up
the little litter of
onomatopoetic anthroponames
to interest the pudding-
headed storm
as it riled the sky's
less than zero
chance to comport
improbably
twisting up chairs
kids sat on to be still.
The squall thrubbed
over afternoon errands;
grass was uncut
from what it complicated.
What more
can be divided
into pairs? A Cozy
Coupe spins off now

in a downpour of light
like paint gone soft
exactly *then*
in *this* new sun. Are
those far Bohemians
impaled
on peaks? Swallowing
magic pictures?
Haled in a breath
from beyond
the pale fence the
instant thought concocts
another rhap-
sodic refugee. Gravity
laughs
without a paddle
as said climber
flows ever sideways
stately up a hill
unfolding then
a siren signifies
"handsomer than
nightfall" and sooner
self-made
untotal
against a handrail leading lightly
to a mouthhole in a tree
revealed briefly as agony
then tender
opportunity
taken on the lip as a knock
histrionic and
from there
full blown

RIOT IN AXIOM

Life is a ball I begin *e pluribus*
     on a bus
   splendid in a hair or lapsed statue
               of grass
raising a fist to wave say
          to Lenin's Lincoln
Continental Nothing new but "a rose
     it's raining and fine"
  in the notorious words of a private
          idealist Possibly
     it can't be true
     the doctor of conditions is finally
   dead at the door
dawn slides back a crack
        young again on a penny
   and to the republic on which the feint
          persists
beyond the drop of a sheet
          (Barnum's seething routine in a cave—
   maddening, predictable, and
          politically incorrect)
               bravos

   Lightning is lobed
  in an all-night grotto
   from which we eventually rain
          squinting homely at the sun
     (anomaly on a chain)
     at the end of which a shot
                              or
   Whistles blow WE ARE NOT
        bondmen on the take
   AFRAID of Sensational Old Generals

O then seize me
            parity
I will be small among the small, a little
            little fellow
        about to walk the line lightly
    disappearing among the avenues
        behind a smoky line of firs
    facing backward

Considering dynamite tonight
            I believe
    I'll go home to my volcano and sleep then
            again as though solo
in a stadium collapsing with metrical feet
            under the wavering compass needle of defeat
    There are people in the street

Berlin, Paris, London, New York, Melbourne
    nothing can bring back the mid-
                                    hour
    of a blow to the head with its
        thickly settled hair
        tossed into jail at the drop of a hat
    and the dead hero can be no deader here
        in my reenactment after the fact
    I substitute sun on the move for the gory flower
            heaving to a zither (contents under
                pressure)
        from conclusion to proposition
    as logical a nakedness in fact as
        a fact of a person in prison
        pajamas

Don't be sad, say "Suck up!"
    you "succeeding happy millions"

to a house full of dubious chits
  about to be tossed
      on the ear of a street leading back
to the hall of records, the time-lapse sap, the foamy
          milk So much
    of the ultimate horizon is sublimated
  if not distressed
          never coming to its sun
          heckled sweet to me
          "And to all states not free"
  I swear I've never met The Man
      for whom the writ
          does not recur
          wide in wood like a nickel
where buffalo play
    unwieldy at the end then suspended
    over a drop
    we may or may not walk away from

WHITMAN

Who goes there ... ?

And so I began to write these lines of dollar operas, plays, and birdsong
Now the sun falls free and smoking
Sane from towers repeating on the rivers one passes down to the East
Across the Alleghenies on the way by car to the beach
Wrapped in sheet music to see how the sea lies
Then seeing by ear how the song plays itself out of a bearded shell
Held up lonesome to a canal soon to be boarded by a pearl and handed
Into the waiting arms of a president

A girl takes the part of the sun, then sun apart
Yet her sequences fade away on wild-farmed apples busheled off
Digital to Rome (upstate) a dime-hard American free to think her
Wordless happy play in doses
Bending hectic eyes wide open
Over backyards under Jupiter
And back again once optimism sets in
Plutonic rocks explode
I am a man of instant sorrow
No longer but a buttonhole on
Fate, lost in an aisle of pomade

As if to sing this labor of latex, my dirty left indexical
Scratches the names of depressed towns along the line one at a time
Into the bark of my own end soap
I am the decay trace of a single moving point of light
Not broadcast but humming the condition of sitting in situ
On the steps of a caboose shuttling away to California via Mannahatta
I dream the name Naima entwined with mine in a hideaway
On a mountaintop of men in hats among some eco-correct plant
       matter collected by
Thunderball, Mother of Us All, queen of nuance on a copycat breeze
She makes joy (the science) stand up to her acquisitions. And, yes, she warbles.

Spring thunderheads drive yardbirds to cover where Pierre Lunaire
is getting settled with his brother Harry Lumber
But the cymbal alone
is never alone a lie

And from a tourist trumpet area I'm joined on the couch by Bibles
Because after all news travels slow over waterfalls
From an original adverbial pinhole on a plain horizon
To a *Man with a Movie Camera*
Billowing down avenues as long as he can stay in the eye
As residue and survive the curse of being always on the way
To the tableaux vivants of a Bunch plucked Wild at random from myself

If you travel, try my brand, my graph of a glyph hanging hankering after
Erie and indigenous before the wind stops dead at a cliff end
And we will agree on nightfall effects
That are of course entirely out of the fountainheads of the last
Jerkwater towns of blab but before that
Let's circulate along the trail by the Mall of the Lake of handsome characters
Cycling through phonebooks laid out in advance of their inhabitants
As they unfold for us the types and faces
Of All Tomorrow's Parties
Then Curtains
So that nothing will be left out of living or something something like it

Like my own clean mother lode, lit up and swinging
Her lamp (and the up-down bird too),
"Whatever happens to anybody"
Will be downright tonic as the soft plopping of wet
Quick gusts shift, sea wraps, whatever happens
This afternoon will be totally different from the first instance and the third
Man Alive in cobalt satin waving a cocktail—model herself citizen and celestial—
And is likely to become Whoever You Are,
Washed up like the rest of us every last day returning restless
To the beach of the borax mines, oh boy. Antideluvial the white soap arrives and I stop

in the middle of pink-barrelled lips to stand down the stampede of
       Know-Nothing explanitives
When the flambeaus of night fall swallowing
When the blackstrap darkens kitchens
Nothing new under the sun rises up aswirl and antisedentary
We forget where we propped our trusty rifles and were
How I could hug them

How my dainty rhymes wrastle sinewy with stripes and stars
I am matter and blood come home to think of whatever fibs are
My fiber will wander (regional) tarnation where I saw the dead boy How
I could hug him aroused in hurried tides of fast-changing terribility
Tarred all over but never tired or sometimes when warbling
A galoot astumble in Reconstruction's woods forever trying to be daylight
       astonished
And not to the decillionth of the other I am

And the backwaters
And the vice presidents
And the teeth of the storm
And the drinking gourd
And the beans
And the fly-balls
And the gentle monitors of meadows and groves
And the portable leather boats
And the boots they bury you in
And the nincompoops
And the bells
And the May bird
And the cypress knees
And the cancer they find
And the probability of change
And the English
And the French
And the Spanish

And the Indian
And the catfish or mullet
And the eating of lizards
And the deserted towns before us and after
And the muckraker and teacher
And the mayor
And the governor
And Miss Pickerell
And the butterfly pea Clitoria
And my young companion, Linus with his afghan
And the scene from the moving train
And the cool of the evening
And the weeding and sorting
And the Floridians
And the generations before me and after gneiss
And the naked
And the jailbirds and jaybirds
And the Linnaeus confusion
And the honk-beepers and honeycreepers
And the flycatchers (all kinds)
And the convenience store
And the banjo button
And Shortnin'
And the Steep Ravine
And the Emigrant Pass
And the capital Snake
And having pretended to know Stein
And the lynch mob
And the Good Book
And the parting
And my worthy old friend
And the other I am not
The same

ENTHUSIASM

Ideas presuppose us
not the head
hand or facture
What is *facture*
the wander of two
shooting the blue
breeze figured in friends
Lull and Hum
Clam and Grass
ear to foot and finger
to ground the word
world
haunting the sky red
and blinking
comes disclaimed the size
our bodies are
plus one
hysterically numbered
now standing in
a short row
whose tune lasts
til newts disband
or originality proves
our idea
in the first place

Pace yourself she says
folding down the beds
wiping her corroded
lips Turn curly
oak for passers-
by to feel then fold
up in leaves as kids

blast
feeling trees
wreaking wrongs
party animals
on the move again
masses mad
to the next motel
uneviscerated still
yet too busy
with fancy cries
or the odd pendulum
out to kill bold
or heal the optimistic
doctor

Then what
shall feeling follow?
A dark hack looking up
electrical calling
a lone peony
spectacle or *scientific outburst*
that clears the air
for ever more
material?
Mud makes a happy
suck where we walk
self-inspecting its flowing
feeling and phenomena
like bees we
get along Don't
go alone into the ego
straining to blot
out the sun It
can't without
aunts enjambed and

whistling longish
verses on a Western theme or
souvenir of its capital
letters whose residues
lead meanderingly
like a simile
up a wash

Leave your honest
mother on her broken
lips we say and seek
a more delicious teacher
typecast herself
to wake hard cold
sure on the shore
of a school
hubbub
where lights gulp
before gushing
and eyes leak
dirigible ghosts
pat pleonasms
striking cataclysms
breaking ground for
a mall of the busy
future to appear
out of the Pecos of not
nowhere now
holding *me* up to the light
as if to prove "Ah,
Poor Bird!"
some of the sum of my
peroration

Collaboration? *I*

doubts it goes without
napping in the car
of thinking these
things or rather
they think you
if time in fact
flows logically back
from any denouement
adding up as it does
to a soft chantey
of lips clapping
somewhat suggestive
of bonafide jaws
going on somewhere
among the larger species
blocked by clouds

The worm lives
just long enough
the wisdom went
craving time alone
a biomechanical wonder
a voiceover cracks
shooting the daily
grind off a cliff
face onto
our own little figures
below nowhere to
go determined so
to cultivate every last
inch
as far as the eye
would if it could
see a dear
friend dear friend

in lieu of whom
a native helps us loop
the loop along
and get the hang of
wrists wrung
on a nudish scrabble
slope left quivering
then to dash
crude notes under a bush
(in the time it takes
the logos to reload)
where a sky swells curtailed
proleptically
out of hand before
another blows in
to replace it and we
give ourselves up
to its blue partitions
Calm and Sung
friend and friend
tied to the tracks
staring down the parting
shot *What?*
nothing if not
ready and hot
with a comeback

IMAGINATION

Poppies prepare buckets
up to be astonished
balancing the way
anyone thinking fills
dewdrops with slow
honey lets bees fly
from silver bullets
hitching the humming-
bird up first as a mistake
then series
of little images and I
remember well
suspenders set
for a spell on a hill
powder flash in a
pan of techniques where
it isn't dull to sit still
perched to curl
operative to a fault in
the forever face
of whatever form
a flower takes
resolvable
in its own premonition

Real drops rain
(momentary states)
irritate local grubs
elementary children
redound hamfisted
to kids redundant (extremes
while they last) abounding
with longing to lounge

only later occurring
as a roar indelibly fine
living the line
from me to whoever's
democratic future's
dead to the world
receding on the waves
of some high-speed
fiber-optic flap to the capital
almost purely alphabetical
as the strobe effect
ties a neighbor
moving behind a board
fence to a mechanical
diary keeping track
of the species—
One calls and I
hustle

Nothing is finer than
facts last night
of a front blows first
of a season instantly fragrant
the unimpeachable debris
of extraordinary acts
disrupts ordinarily re-
fractable solos exactly
above and to the side
as stylus to overture
a tone before
the world divides
into subjects and heads
nodding with sun the sum
of particles and waves
falsely at angles of ease

individuals and their images
sciences and their parents
those geniuses whose fractions
propagate sheer crush
like us para-
plenipotentiaries
milk flat on a stone fills
and the flat fear is
it will fall

Late I awoke
perched with a hitch
in my gitalong home
on the waves
of granular robustness
lay awake reckless
left and right tethered
to a pinpoint replica
honey at rest
the day remains
how hot it will get
predictive an itching
disrupts smooth
solos on a field
continuing on
unseen from the road
to an urgent antipodean
imaginary leaning bravely
ungainly on ladders
to an individual boy
with a real request

Forced down bravely steeped
in images composed
in motions I check the

time fix lunch
board a bandwagon in the teeth
of the onrush of a rescueless opposite
in the continuous arising of a tree
next to a box emblematically
boulders along
breathing leaning long
like any self-confident narrator
life can never be lived
executive
on the other side of the mountain
signal to noise
nose to stone
ear to there
at once the report
here and clear and close.

HAT SCHISM

For I would not be a slave if I could help it under a hat the lack of whose shade would leave me smart naked in the rain. For what I want are dry pants and an early start tomorrow. I hate the unreaped field, its over-reasoned surplus now doffing to a dream of opposability. For it is an indolent sinking sun falling on the fox I admire alone in hiding. Do I sing too loud? I am a child who's forgotten all about it, but having heard the forbidden anthem begin to long for home again myself. For any god's quantity of fiddlers you may make up a feather bed I'd be glad to lie in. For I am composed of calculation and little holes. For this land is my limb. Such are the unravished prisoners the larks these states—

L et us march. Let us have blankets and let us have our instruments. Let it be tomorrow, dubiously. Plunking down our two bits after washing up, us boys get out on the sly and try to have a damn good time. Let the moguls have their clams and the hullabaloos their athenaeums of salted meat blandishing the bounty of the woods; if only the Green River flowed black eternal to the rain on the left and the rain itself held us up as models. Let the bird in the hat play dice and wait. New orders are sure to take me from here. Escape? Let the fool attempt it; I won't—

For like a cork I float on delusion at the end of which the bear-wife returns on the word, *Honey?*—remembering an interesting chat back in the woods on Kansas Matters. I have sewn up my own mouth with iron thread not to say slaughter. But I have forgotten to whom this song is addressed, for I am as lonesome it is said as the devil left on a battlefield where I am little more than an interval, a fool who lay with a cloud fondling the sweet illusion of a hill from this valley they say, for I expect we will all die yet—

L*et* the mail come in then and bring me a letter. Damn near froze last night. Now it's time we took the E-flat tuba out in the woods and practiced marching and countermarching awhile. Let us look into the pond for Armitage's body standing dead upright next to a whale for which we'll have no good explanation, then I'll get some coffee and bacon (them too an illusion) and swim on in the drench. Thus early I learned the point from which a thing is viewed is of some signal importance. Darn thumb. A hellhound follows *Taps*. Who can say how long I'll sit wet on my adz waiting before the instruments arrive at last but only after a Mr. Hale of Company H dies in hospital. Let this stanza offer (*a*) interim defeat in a dream or (*b*) parley strange; *I'll* wager victory up the pike—

For we must disenthrall ourselves from our sleepy mothers and their unhappy misnomers. Queens of Memphis, dyspeptic Kings. What victor, what madman, what poor cuss shall we celebrate? For water has turned to ooze in the camp faucets and there is no powder to calm the stallion's mood. Bad stomach? Disrelish. After a good deal of gassing with Harve & Charley retired for the night on my hard bed & so closed the year 1861. For what's done is did, though I still love these towns on the way to Jezebel. After that, I could not say if I woke or slept for all the powder in me, for I left the continuous world by daylight—

*L*et the shot fall deaf on the farms of farmers where the rain might rise up to meet or fend it off, since I am spilt in the drains of my heart. Let me just make it to Cincinnati where a steamer lies none the wiser. Since I'm hardly a profound metaphysician and can barely give tongue to my defection my indirection will be more than discreet. Let the ferns uncurl humble under needles in mud now that Zallicofer is defeated with 400 of his dead defeated men also and all of his artillery. Bilious gasses haze the corn moon and I've departed from my company at last bootlessly regretting the glue of the man made of me. Let them beat the bushes. The trees are not dead. Let their hair stand on end—

For the salmon is a silly fellow creature, one of great personal instinct but some confusion, a dry-witted cuss lying in the river declaiming MAD TRAGEDIAN COMES TO OUR CITY and in my hunger I believe him or her. For I am too thoughtful to be happy in escape from dawn of dusk to day of dark keeping hard to the woods working my way along the emptying miracle stars. For I was engaged in a great incivility, and had as well be killed running along alone as die standing in the middle. I remained all night in life—sleep I did not. I must compose myself. For when I finally get to Town [applause] folks will little note nor long remember the return of my great personal father dark abashed at having found me in this awful state—

A*nd* when the great carnal gnat cried into the bell of the girl waiting on my recovery I cried too, Let me go back to the farm hat or some mail-order other 100% billet or ballot or scroll to win my applause [applause]. Let Pericles praise the buck stalled in the woods eyeing us (O foolish hectic) every week the *Liberator* came and I made myself the master of its contents, owner once more of my own triple refrain. We cannot hallow this Kentucky ground any more than Darke is a County true fitting and proper for free happy forebears who dwelt nowhere verily but in their socks. I look out on the union of an idea. Soaked. All men [applause]. All women [applause]. For I am new here in these plosive pairs. Please. Let the notion born from a proposition be formed in a living sound that shall not perish, probably, shall not inherit the asterisk clause. The procedural is processional and shall rise up to stand on its two hind legs, vice and versa, here or hereabouts [long continued applause].

Otium

ROMANTIC FRAGMENTS

or if it thinks, farewell. Only this eight remains

of a house on fire in the thick
of a wandering band of offhand physicians
whose radiances don't end at the end
of the earth or edges of the eyes where
their effects peel away to original metal
or petal after all in spring. The why of ice
over a kind of belief. Not
the really *big* piece. To make one
alive (a goose loose in a gale) or two even more. What is important
is to do something in the present

with as many fingers. Everything can be said

but let's sing it instead!—becomes the de facto summer
of the will to thunder in a latent O
in turn expressing a slippery grappling
while we synthesize our own antipodes
asking what distance separates the model Sally
from the copy Ann—the grime
of the hand—it can go either way—a sacred
or secular cloud drained of dollar
bills but cool as a rose stands still at any crossroads. A given, or simply some
internal apostrophe?

on the way to earth. The crude cosmopolitan is

like me, finite on the way to infinity, is why
the boomerang wind (there, I said it again), is *how*
revolution hates eruptions
of the past, commuter train
in its own mouth. My [illegible]
ukelele's broke on a North
we neither know nor lament
since suffering the cruelty of rust, the zip
fastener acts out its increments, ever smaller
coded instructions spooling inside her

the world presupposes. Not a bridge for the not

so antisocial, stretching her wide arms
as flags or figments of possible touch knocked
off the blue example marked Exhibit
Anthem. We laugh like addicts then
make the ASL sign for "but" to let
"the little work of art" win. Off the mower
our glad but flawed procedures reflect a simple fellow
feeling, having cracked the door
with a wooden shoe, the one
I meant to keel us over

into the double daydream. Caesura

forms around a glitch
or ditch in which one spring you learn
your replacements have been planted. No one knows who
started taboo, or whether they're in or out.
You put your lip on the lip
of the broken whatsit, but it's the child you always meant
to mean. Beyond the bend you just see
her miniature finger
point. The song trills up, swings back;
I wish there were more

love in proper names. Hopeless detours

refer us to the votive character of memory
staked by good-hearted interns who earn less
by sensuous presentation than
does the intimate Teflon of a suit
of amnesia reborn as a gorgeous girl. All the days
in the world don't add up
to opera. Your name here
insofar as it is in play. Rumor
coincides with her caption, "what
lies basking in the sun," and the touching implied

hearing the swamp rise. The sky was all over them

as if there were no sun to take its place: The much maligned
pig, her mouse and his wolf—all breeders now
in the museums nature leaves
tisking on the breeze, none has time
to eat the other. Geniuses pony on
alone to therapy. Two in the bush dust themselves up
watching the propeller plane drop down
for an antique landing. Can word of mouth
be eaten? The distressing illegibility
of the noisy air. To live is

ensemble. Not bad, but too late

like any answer nine inches by three inches by
twelve feet deep my mouth is so dirty
you can taste the money
and hope Houdini—whose hair got away
but whose suit stood firm—
returns free to a clearing for those of us who look on
at his back and for those others waiting
the forest streamed up and spoke the epic everything,
absolutely, that had already happened

complete in itself. Charismatic animals in a tableau

stare. One pig gets a whiff of a storm
on the brain (medically, the gumming-up of cells) and winks
before extending a hoof to the chase. A robust and fabular
melancholy is the absent father
of these unprivate thoughts, who nods internally
to the tabula nuda of exotic time expanding
until enormous of course unfixed
in the skin of a book. The one you retire to begin. If you manage to return
come as a fragrance
or not at all

to the Vermilion Tower. Pure pleasure

sees. Lies in second thoughts. Tear out the sky
and do it over so at least one of us can renew
what we already know. Made conscious
by the sonorous complex of bonafide space extemporaneous
the young pods
learn to speak
so the world might be saved from speculation
and the irascible dictates of replication
under the penetrating gazes of its many monster
mothers

nailed on the spot. Even breathing

is awkward after a conviction. These three-
legged chairs used to be for milking but here
I've made little handled bargains
just to sell. Let down your ropy ladder hair
on the way out we'll say to sweep away these substandard toys
and put to rest this interest
in paradoxes once
and for all. "Muscular" said of no one in particular after
the sun fell
as if guarding some swank interior life

with neat disguises. Lift the eye

away from its perspective
squandering its interior in a mass
of tentacular sentences and soon enough
another war—excuse me, "action"—will arrive in a waver (cough)
between travelogue and communiqué: tree farm
or windbreak? Just the kind of diversion you'd expect
armed to the trees
with teeth. These utopian proposals
having foundered on a final orifice
for whom we're always the last drop; nothing in the world

would let us in. The mother explains

everything promptly spins out
having come to a town near the boat landing
and looking back so humid the pale
precedent a hard rain
of *the real thing* filling up vessels like us
erotically bound to fall apart in the world
that is a condition of denatured fit.
"Yesterday!" we exclaim, locked like plums in someone
else's refrigerator; it could never have been better
than good enough

as the crow flies. Two days later

imagine a parallel world of similar stature: "Good
aim!" says the Green Man falling down
preemptively dead at the site where everyone knew
the two armies would anyway eventually converge
and so begins the draft from red
to greener. I lie coursing in bed thinking back
to side I can't leave you two
(three) names to bleed. English
is elegiac crickets opine and time feeling
fails

to discourage the world from concerning itself

with us. The game begins with a verb, *to bear*
witness or swoon so the little boot that bobs
on a postindustrial lake
will always know its mother: FARM
HORN MOB PASTE (NOT
BE). She is an example
of the circle round the sun when it
becomes a god and what a wit
miles from the nearest dot or ammo cache then
having earned hard scrabble

on a dare. Now that's a condition

Do I wake like a house on fire or do I
slope in waves? Sleep? None to be had.
A television, disappointed, say, at finding itself so
struggles to die, waves good-bye
in the distance where rubber armies dissolve
in simple fascination with their folded paper weapons.
Unslept I am frequently visited by this illusion:
you outrun your shadow to get naked
in my arms (you splendid girl, infinity
is in you!)—it is my own, a widening pool

pronominal, spilt. It was not to interest society in myself

that I took these odd positions, but to enchant.
I didn't want to cool thinking down
with a sponge, so I spit out a tooth
to make room for a speech
that might serve to solve
the riddle of what is always promised and full
as soon as it is leveraged
A precise calibration of polar dews
I sit down to write
in the name of a drop in the bucket: zero

flexing its shapely index. A person's false end

It would not be incorrect to speak of my imagination
but why on earth? I'd divide my slips
into peel or pearl, plus or minus one; neither cows nor hands
seem to mind the quotes. Forget diction; you might die
watching television unable finally to ask
and is art nothing? Blank is *blanc*
is an overstatement, lyric
flayed. So let's make a monument
to the cheap parts (someone might still be living there) and anyone
made uncomfortable by all the holes in me

or any son of a gun. These untamable creatures

deify a perfectly nice pair of—genitalia out of this world!
As, reaching from a zero point to the topmost apple,
they see themselves split, a linguistic problem
but a turn-on too, a unit of bliss stuck in the fear
of losing one's own eyes. Buster Keaton checks his pulse
then ear again to hear the ant shout, "The perceptible emperor
is a greedy man! Turn him into a big wild pig!"
Well, the ability to turn tail and run wouldn't be so fearsome
if two were one rock solid. *Or,*
the best ethical position can be compared to an egg

up a ladder. But the real anxiety arises

from repetition, like an important sleeper, whose dream
is poked by a pin on the chair of the absolute
teacher (didn't she feel anything?) and then resumes
in [expletive] explanations. The return of the same
day in, day in ... the story speeds up
with the noise of a big dumb machine and so on into the night. She was,
you might say, completed in the end, having worried the link
with her mother (off in a burrow or dead
somewhere), an uncanny apparition of an unmoored
infant, waiting to be with you

of all people. The whole of the dull, dark, soundless day

organized underground I remember
thinking It was like a bee
to a jar
of money foretold by a person who said
she saw something sweet down
the swallowing subway having lied about the bag of bones
shifting in her niche
having lived more or less forever on the lam
in a country where it never rains
Revelation? No such place

as a belly of water. Riled

while I was away. The sky opened up again, dropping
a new antidote down. The people were to "collect
themselves," but wasn't that a contradiction in terms?
Surrounded in a valley by troops on all sides
the overtold, underobserved password was the body
(you don't *wear* technology, you live it!) each had on.
It couldn't be explained
having written nothing before Nobody conceived
the image of an ancient important torso asleep
under siege. Not to equivocate but to proliferate

since it is easier to make art than to live. The principle

arrives, like the colonizer
to her unwilling host, all water under a bridge over
a border beyond lives lived entirely
unknowable by some super-omniscient "us."
You might be the one they call Mimic Master
Man, sorting through a bilious overflow of artifacts
and throwing these up as signs across
a chasmy landscape that is otherwise something
of a predicament. So saying, one's easy divinity might be dinged
by a dusted-off thunderbolt. But is the "so" coordinating or resumptive—

ambivalent liquid rippling? If bad sands turn

new leaves—that's optimism—
anterior painted over in a posterior rose. When
the insatiable public demands a new frontier say
look under your shoes you river of dubious red;
integrity is a reckless remainder of the vanishing
creams of the shore where the head is strong but a fragment
imploring impeachment if not secretarial detachment.
But immediately the question arises [the professors turn their phrases
to face us], is it important
to entertain the bohemians of an unoccupied future?

as when, for instance, having decided to regale myself in a prison cell

minutes under canopy blue pop like diary droplets
of mental material escaping frame by frame out the door down
the drain around the block. It's the present that lingers, the stutterer
will start to say because suffering can't be treated categorically
or undersold by just any licensed doc. We recoil from our own tall
tale even as we concoct it, an abduction
subtended from even flimsier invention, where our delegate
digits sleep curled up (as if in a bunch on a branch)
waiting for a break. Is there no authorized text
in the internal theater? Not in ships or on foot

will you find the marvelous road. An accordion turns

on devotion, echo of its love for folded air, a bright idea
arriving to take form. As if the shore were not already
more than sufficient for a family of three
players, a trace of my blood is always pushing beyond
the closed position, the future that lies open
in the next chamber always already mixed
up with chance over-
come with emotion not unlike cement in solution or bark cut
from a tree stitched into a boat carrying its person
to the games of the people of the north. What is it

that blends with the words and so to speak

animates them with weeping? Min-Xu, our young voice
has vanished and the song off the pool's almost icy.
Whitman begins as a tonic ends
apotropaic; could she have gone off to learn fear
(a story in which I, as her mother, play a minor part
like in a parade where you get to ring a triangle no more
than once)? But the breast is its own shade
an umbel not a clump
and we (dissenters) dissent
before *chump* can be written in our albums

with metered sadness. Whence indeed

an important metalepsis came. Where do we go
from here? To a substitution that is usually incorrect
and the call to evening roulette
whose interest attaches us to what is not
ourselves but our everyday lapses. Retract the scalp
to let go a smile—the feeling fellow feels the rigging ting
in a breeze along the hurtling burnway, prototypical
harrow in a furrow suprasensible
(with an index guide to all the supplements)
the ductility of biography nothing equals

or liquid half. Unaware that she was on a volcano,

laboring happily her whole life—or anyway one morning.
In the athenaeum—it was intriguing but profitless
her mania for itemization, particulation; could happiness
be reduced to a list? an open horizon of relations
both speculative and retrospective?
or a crater, into which a great scathing wind pours
the sense of obligation we all felt
at one time or another as if a cataract into a thimble or tiny cup, far
from the nearest thoroughfare, itself figured
in the brightness of the movable world? Is it in the lavish swimming halls

where most of the plot eddys? The plane of the horizontal

is desublimatory, a container for the ebb
and flow of motion, a setting for spillover
into the ideal chemistry or body-
world in which your cracks can be laughed at—not just understood
but easy to ape in the mist of fugitive
Sullivans on the take amid the axiomatic self-satisfaction
of subjectivity. Why do kids across the fence sing
a song about the planets? It's a job with a funny
far end. The corpse is a hoot
in cartoons, but *I* am a chain-gang fugitive

pursued by sounds of the axe. Voice!

a synthetic expression emanating directly from the idea
of a forest of something other than trees
picking up steam in a suburb of the brain
overcome with variation and unusual duets
carrying on like Indians of a new non sequitur
ripped from the hats of their enraptured visitors
Audubons themselves snowed in under a pile of debts
when Tin Pan Alley's nocturnal nightjar
by name, sitting cousin to a mechanical duck—
A little sparrow with two strange rudders, the whippoorwill

wouldn't dream of it. Puns

do something in the present. Following
these melodic shapes
in devolution ("On earth, I too …"),
a particularly thorny line from Lincoln
("The sound should carry," he said
into the noise of the machine, "like water over
rocks"; but secretly to me: "Then why is it *humans* who
are always bawling?"). The blank slate isn't the punctual sky,
in other words, whose outward clouds enclose you, mute
and smokeless but (naturally) us, a database

that words arouse. Rain will fall fast

if only one could paint her left buttock blue
leaving the other to dangle in the wind over a perilous drop
stunt day into stunt night etcetera
executed by a Toon, say, flattened by her fall to a natural state. What exists
now, after all, is a powerful market for definition
bracketed by competition, I mean computation, a divine work-station
obstetrician and embodiment of twilight. Who says the world is no longer
enchanted? The quotation starts and falters, self-important, flat-
footed, looking back on itself as "a boundary of the permissible
in the empire of sound." "Rain or the rope!" shout

the wardens. Forget that you are monsters

on a waterfall where the original sensitive and animate
friends were stranded, this part, of course, becoming
more beautiful for the sound of the oars before
one of us jerked, "Triceratops!" And as if melody were indeed
antilyrical I had to ask what *about* smoke
gets in your eyes? Gravediggers await
those who sing too much and the rest of us meat-eaters
and vegetarians line up accordingly to take our places in the mechanical
orchestra called by social scientists and their funders
"a zoo of unexpected particles and reactions." But our secret is

more than alive. Apollo hunted Daphne so

the metaphor of the mind at sea or as one
could be folded up and kept in the pocket of a jacket
you might wear on a walk downtown to the opera or in this case
up as a reminder of signs
impossible to decode. Getting you where?
Which war was it that was over?
By choosing to join the march (your toe clapped sadly
shut in homogeneous empty time—sandwiches
but no drinkables) you're strung up in a locution
made of gum and *dilatio*. Infinite but not perfectible

the verb implies swelling. An anthill is not impossible

to replicate, conception being mostly acting
in particulars. So one doodles on
as the engineer inside fuses limbs into larger
and more important questions. First I just wanted to build
landscapes like myself, then a lionlike person
boarded the train challenging my conviction in realism
and although I soon saw the moon hanging fire
as the foreground sped away as if from jail
I was not afraid
but a dramaturge

struggling to get into my own sentence. Beauty deposes

itself in institutionalized forgetting
what strange rain falls on the earth
among visions of whirlwinds and someone
hitting me up for change
daily draining and filling hard the eyes
and ears of friends render the sun
down and like ponds can be trolled
or bathed in as days and nights are organized
into knockout pairs until the first
person returns and a handout is really all

she has to go on. From afar in my heart

the sonic bath resumes. This mother
it would be fair to say didn't crave separation
but sleep will overtake any bonded pair then
a quick snort provides the shock a simple knock
to the head couldn't accomplish, which,
now that I was awake, meant I had rhythm
and no one could stop the hand-to-hand of the fire
brigade all shouting at once but responding to no apparent
prompt. An echo went off in a "filthy sack,"
systole on windfall—what was the word? Skin

thanks to this reduplication? At night all cows are black

in fact, I look down at my skeptical hands waving
their feelings for the stars in the fantasy of daylight—
itself a phenomenological mistake it is normally impolite
to depict like eclipses when for example the insides
of *The Blob* might be spilling out onto a sham diurnality—
and a reporter who's supposed to know (or find out)
how it works not to know (but she's a youngster and so
extratemporal) is struck flat by her own fanaticism
ticking. My head in *her* hands detached (as a rider from its horse)
only a skip in time and as they say all nerves lead away

to the ranches of dawn. There is excess

like a baby bellowing in the woods, for example. Sacrifice entails
the mind's fall to jaws green
with juice and handy bright monitors
claim full disclosure frankly
a relief to us novices still handsome enough to wax
uncynical if what the hands accomplish
is so small and havoc so dear
two or more bodies may slip into what else
but a dark night where the sun *will* shine as recto
to this verse. Speak your solution but it is nearly

insoluble. It's easier to compose

like the earth to a footstep if
young blades of grass yearn up local
to anthems about to be sung by a nation imagined as pieces
of eight, then eaten, worked
in the interval between comedy and idol
and as if the free use of any foot
was natural the tide
of commerce subsides over the berm as another day
(or delegate) blends with the crowd and moves on
Why was I in such a hurry anyway to buck

a miraculous branch? So, my friend, into a hubbub

the prolapse of waiting for a reason to come
clear. Buffalo Bill put his money on Laugh Cream,
The Great Lung Healer; for us it's all one
big bucket of, dare I say—I don't dare say. Alertly
adaptive and widely recursive he reaches
his imported hand out to canvas the once-mountain stream for what it
was, a stanzaic meditation on making do. So
with a soda in the other and a way of "singing
in his own head," Bill met me recovering
from the strange and wonderful history

nothing stands still to witness. A process with no necessary end

exiled in the sun. Got up, felt dubious
in the tedious accumulation of nothing important
nothing bungling nothing erratic and I sometimes hoped
as they say in the sea
for a volcanic eruption of gorgeous arrows flying
from a string of once and for all gentle thoughts
Was anyone ever actually "handsome in triumph"?
For the sand in domestic jars
can't be counted and the future tense
refers to nothing outside the present. The free agent

smokes. We picks up where I left off

in every matter, measure. But you are full of it
matter, I mean. "Water, upon which waves, upon
which a bundle of sensitive particles, woman or
ventrical through which the spectacle of a capital Man rocks the touch
of the free radical at a hard
time." Yet it is not so co-eternal with you
this most ridiculous structure
fallen on latex and line
this the case is (she or he)
who always stands where a beginning was

OTIUM

I do not innovate! —Noah Webster

To a green thought in a green shade the chase always ends in the
scribbled corrections of an Updraft the secret flutes and Trumpets
of which (if only in the Rhombus of an Idealist's hairy eye) take the form
of resistance in a hand Stuck out to hail a runaway blowing the Whistle
on a form on fire through a scrim behind which free lunch and sex all the
time are the Peacable problematical terms for everything lackadaisical
that had come to pass away Raw and material but the crows of repletion
still echoed back then from onomastic hills Uncontainable and the elders
piped up periodically from their continuous internal Logbooks Nodding
when Integers appeared on the horizon that was the beginning of the
infinite series historical time was for idle Heroes and the countering
countdown Upright to humans the air mostly clear there with days and
nights published regularly in Pairs but always partial to One or the other
you had to ask not how much but how Sweet It Is to fly in the face of
a deadpan ringer while the wake from our Whaler Roared up behind
as it died away it bloomed again with infatuation as the Sum of one
hand sketching a Fragment and another the words that words Arouse in
anyone Thinking personally

Namely Daylong it was probably irrelevant but in the Lavish cold
swimming halls before the great march of Dimes I saw now what
could not reasonably have been sung then by the first person Viridian
the skinks and chameleons massaging the fontanels of brand new earth
seeding itself and Erupting unpredictably both far and near with Bossy
choruses the Question was was it good to be Ebullient or even sentient
responsible to a world returning the favor and a Wanderer the kind
who's forgotten the note in her hat that says where she set out from
over hill and Dale and Parenthetically the sea though few yet existed
wanderers not hats for there was no committee work only a Deck
chair and that loaded in your favor on a stack of Unread magazines sat
progress the figs always molded before they could be read with Relish

and eaten then great schools of fish came Puncturing our conversation
irreproducible as it was with us paddling noiselessly as if into a
wonderful Cliché

And we having lives to live returned to our sweeping if only to
remove the Dead swelling in mounds of somebody's Somebody
over sunk towns and so on without compensation for memory was
preprogrammed like sleeping but not weeping Exactly over the souring
cities with their curious peaches yet collapsing as the bough breaks when
sitting at your desk (budding) the teacher one day naturally rational
would come along to pour a Handsome but Deadly emptiness in but you
were already full of it whistling the melody to yourself of the Cut that
comes down inside the Head and sloping to the sea (sad "Dixie")

From which a *heimlich* Homeric tradition spun dappled from nymphs
and infants fattened on the backs of Bad Agriculture and the
husbands who told it sold it off like grass Grass could be hay anyway
it would grow like a Debt before the crop wilted as if film having
miniaturized the horizon in the keyhole of a letterbox wanted it both
ways a wife running off from the Mob in her aversion to matronization
ends up Barrel-rolling on a prairie weirdly happy but it can't Last because
the Movies decompose in ever more diminutive diminuendos sewing
seeds that turn to Credit later if not to a card

Hauling great capitals into Position it was the command of a
sleeping dream Indigent and Actuarial that I go to get money
from a Wall and date it for the archives later when somebody's leisure
Chair would be bent back double and the stubble fields would set their
Silhouettes up along Estuaries for reenactments with Souvenirs of
all the great battles living and being Interrupted the names of things
Flourishing deafening the Disarray though the conversation would never
Flag under the smell of Wet willow it was better than a sceance with the
typical metaphysical Expatiation on Tears and by association trees that
exude sap will be the onomatologist's work but her Hand was stretched
out still

What more could we want beyond Maintenance with cigars the rain fell fast without words it Never has words you say but the Discrepancy belongs to an arithmetic mistake I always make (like an expatiation on tears) that Imagination could deliver us from what we Contemplate in other words the beautiful Droplet probably can't be consumed in the Saccadic movement of the saddle-sore eyes of an increasingly Interested neighbor who might Snatch physical pleasure out of the Jaws of Death or defer it Loping off to work instead at the lab where the presses churn on Dumb to the Stickiness of trees whose knowledge if they knew would only deepen their Pertinence

But that's how one referred to sex or Exit Data then as if like Butterflies skippers saturniids noctuids and geometrids we all sought a "perfect Shape" and not just in our own minds but face to face in Legislation where even there and then it was not such a crime to exoticize and therefore Love unattainable Captains like the little Hoot owl who works staying up days Whetting silver wings in the secret police as a Subindex of our hirsute Hairshirts and their territories swaying without rhythm but erotic nonetheless If anyone remembered that Last fact of Life none of us would have been sent to ride in a car across a plain to have that one thought about space that made ourselves the condition of it and almost Phreatic but also pedagogically Apt for those of us who caught a glimpse of the Yellowlegs eyeing the mail-plane's shapely Pontoons as if someone were taking us there Anyway in a song

Be happy the husband called things that are Little don't remain so the rain doesn't fall it Feels (cheaply like quotes quoting themselves openly Soma drinking the last Drop of Herself) if you ask politely you'll never be In but cut for cut the day is yours like Mine elastic as Bees and botany employing the Method on the grandest possible scale Jambed up here and there of course but you do grow and move on in great backfiring Twists attaching yourself as it were to the bright Peduncles of flower and fruit in the manner of a limpet but Thirst of a Clam as time passes and it would Even Here show me the Hasp of your lock you advised therapeutically and I'll Fiddle with it and show me the Back of

your face and I'll fix that too as you Know it was headhunters then who
single-mindedly waxed our corners smooth meanwhile the Mind fell on
grass Us we just chewed the bright Fern quietly logaoedic that is calm
as dust feigning disinterest in the open Phylacteries they stood quietly in
front of waiting to see how our Paradiddle descending into Night might
or might not Proceed

You see we had choices panic Possibly pain even there in the realm
of Euphoric radical revisionism where our cadres of Ladies in
families multiplied and no one who could would dare to stop us from
spreading out our beach or breach towels separately under the Platted
sky each section its own Pleonasm but not unpleasant or unduly diligent
to the job of waking up daily to the Decision to be happy yet you were
Dogged either way by a baneful zoomorphic Fantasy of dignity one
you might approach perturbatively but without the Physics maybe
that was the distinction between duty and one step beyond to pushing
supplements in a duffel bag full of Wax Beans and vitamins adding an
order of corrections distributed Unequally by consent or free Choice
and with this worry our Ova returned as words like us Adverbum to
the Punctuality of the killdeer's not so unhappy Cry everyone sings too
much complained Debussy his own atmospheric hypothesizing an ordeal
of beginning and end a Plink and that was Then

The Ovidian paradox of it was that a palooka might Change into a
Saint but stay the same in her well-meaning ravings whose irony
will be Revealed in future stanzas of intervening transactions where
Green is a shade almost a draught of liquorish biographical Sustenance
bubbling from a rock face and pooling when You were ready for School
I smoothed out our folding house and went with you for I had Long
forgotten our Getaway coracle tied up and waiting in the metaphor of
the mind as an Ocean and Most of the multiplication table after 6

So that life as they say is for Rileys ready and willing to entertain the
pure bright sidereal Phantasms of unprejudiced Reasons and their B-
sides like the idea that the seas contained exact Replicas of us or flowers

were the spurious shadows of their Fruit whereas *glasnost* changed
almost All of everything after that at least everything on time or in it
and the Bell rang but Clumsily as if knotted by malcontents to a knitting
needle and used to Cow a dropsical chorus so that when you flew away
readers did not wish it Otherwise drained and absent themselves of
Intention or fine-tooling but I did standing Stony unretouched in a fog
that could only be called Glaucous and only looming up

If the orchestra of aliens suddenly Quit we felt we should honor
their Picket because we as good neighbors were Pillars now of those
upon whom we had earlier Experimented and in our "brittle summer
Jackets" coughed a little waiting for some further sign found finally in
the checkered petals of a Happily unfolding tactility the Organs of which
might be Discovered in a pyx or Heap of Busts attractive as substitutes
for an actual corpus otherwise glad like Chaplin in *Modern Times*
defaulting to the Machine for which there is never a Remedy but with
Longanimity coming out fine in The End

And so it went our ships had sailed we Marched into the lighted
dining rooms for Supper some of us asleep some still talking of
infinite perfectibility but lightly as friends Do after Cocktails when
everyone was asked to Sing and we felt the colossal Approach of an
Institution an Inquiry almost Veterinary that wouldn't go away as
later much later we Walked upon the lawns having been Elected for
the Job and having brought along a glockenspiel to mark the fun of
time Incandescent suddenly in the flicker of a surge and our courtship
effervesced again in the air paused Wrestling on the ground returned
glittering to the treetops (there were some then) ending exhausted in the
milkweed fields Dead I suppose but poised in the very middle of the free-
floating First or was it our second ethical question

SIXTEEN LUCKY DREAMS
(Epical Pictures)

Meanwhile night had begun to fall.

ONE (METER)

"Meanwhile in our booth
even a little finger could dream of a crowd
nostalgic and sad like two orioles
attacking one small subaltern
dragonfly off duty on the hand of a former
farmer a dictator reformed
now to simple fusion obstreperous
and genetic a cloud spills perilous
over yellow a dress
sent from pantlegs in exile
hayseeds and all it begins with a dactyl
or aftershock to look up.
But the sky is no place for data."
So saying, the dream is a remake.

TWO (GEM)

Inside the speech meter perked
officially a circus dream and prime
stumbling like the shy elephants
who strode towering to our town in summer
for the tonic. In that new world or tent
it was said by speech
one adopts all poses apple-green
like skin not a part but a condition
external to matter (love) whose ends
make awesome the sky (or weather; the near and far sides
of its discontinued monument)
attached to which an elephant
(now a cow)
stands by a filament
docile for the dawn and a great favorite.

THREE (VISIT)

"Galloping on a mettlesome stallion the visitor
comes home on the rain
falls from the sun just to be fair
to the diligent proofreader of an unusual shade—
blue behind an oxidized door where
individuals trade parts scribbling 'Twas
ever thus' in clownish script
on the blank slates
of each other's backs. There
Magnanimous Despair arrives
great in the ear a verse
fitted with birds, tears, oranges, undergarments, the starchy
sky a heaving sun—all reasons
to hurl the writing instrument away
as the same water travels up and down the crystal tube
day after day."

FOUR (TURNING BLUE)

What strange rain recurs then
silhouetted in mid-air
falls on the last night of a demon
decoy one foot in the air who
adjusting her ankle as a fragment of the beat
disappears begins "What drop
convinces amid scenes of contagious
shooting? Penetrates the tongue and rests there
before anyone can explain
pneuma to us
arrows rain, crumbs legion
I and everyone
set up for instruction?"

FIVE (LULL)

"Rousseau couldn't sit through it without tears
the part on mental anguish being
nothing in particular
an auditory hallucination maybe
of his own blood bosses
whose carnal faxes and their untouchable echoes
billow in from the provinces
of absent discourse
but fail to extinguish our restless will
to get to the bottom of nothing at all
now that you and I are one in limbo and so too
the disputed aria of a certain General Pyramid
arriving out of breath along a dustless grid
amid breezes of a tule lake where
we or he'd disport with our companions
if time would tell (or you could read my minds)
in the salty summer months."

SIX (INTELLIGENCE)

"I was sure I was awake when I set my eyes
a fair distance apart (one projecting beyond
my wiry nose) and leapt up on the only waiting
horse giving chase to a completely logical
stranger or was it she pursuing me to the point
of petrifaction in a sea of sounds and voices to that cul-de-sac
where Johnny Cash (as priest) eats the horse or mummy
saying he's never 'picked cotton' meaning
'let's mine great words and eat the entail'
true tenants
of the days you were born to be wild
[here the horse is directly addressed] and turned loose
on the avenues of the stars in our eyes."

SEVEN (LEAP)

"But I hate poetry" she said retreating
from the broad overlook on a dreamed-up theater
where the sun is born from a Dixie cup for sheer
economy and when her sister suggests
going to the dogs to be eaten she goes gaily
gazing on a greenish average, classical
not classic, possible, not pale, chained
to the rocks between two peaks improbably
a recovering Echo. "Mother of God [or someone's older brother],
can this be the end of Rocco?"

EIGHT (FORM)

The bed being a better esoteric set-up for a functionary to forget in
without addition or subtraction something
has to be done looking in as clouds do
on the residues of our ambushed heroes here
crumpled on a point where canonical landscapes converge
and we can all partake in the blue return
of a salty individual shooting fortified raindrops
to be recognized as stars in a tangle
eternal to the one false move of the art
form of our time. That is,
raising oneself up wholesale
from a nugget to the pantleg of an angel.

NINE (ONE OF THE HOURS)

"Therefore I created the world in a false take
and then (now) the curtain slips not as it was then
when a heavy velvet almost the color of deep
auditorium sleep interrupts the safe progression of miniscule
tasks from dawn to diminution and why should the world
now that it has begun know of its end in pale
sun until it happens to you experience
just wants to burn
pleasantly fat and corseted tight awake I will orchestrate
our 'session' without memory or desire at least
that's how I'll *say* many more beautiful things but I am
on the long road to nowhere special and shall remain
superstitiously opposed to fanfares."

TEN (PINING)

"By some ominous rocks the world restarts
now hard night what shrubbery gives
away reveals a picture of the future
footnote on success bare-breasted I await
my playdate love the migration
of acting to plastic film inside a frame it's
what we've come for the world
derived by some increment kept track of theatrically
with a watch out in new night what foliage
represses where I float awake
in plush the matter we can all prorate
the blue as it arrives open in disarray
crumpling an archaic improv up
in a hand held out to learn
or return to misremembered freedom."

ELEVEN (AUTOBIOGRAPHY OF A *Borometz*)

"The first of all yellow dresses was a mother dragonfly
cramped in her uses from which we agree by arriving
to free her and training up as pups pleated
accordionlike for portable and free expression
a long string of unreliable witnesses dips
from the spinnerets of trivial images dappling
our embroidery of a vivid disquiet as we grow up-
ward able only to look down on the grass that once
nurtured us needles in hay declined against
each new seduction the sun itself packs up
a little ditty bag of stuff for three journeys to seven lands
of proliferation, nametags (with portholes) for every one
of us who wants one to set out in."

TWELVE (PERILOUS NIGHT)

"I noticed my head was leaking
into the sac of an undisclosed sea
area unwatched as a disc spun hidden
among the branches of a wading dream like a lamp
burning inside a tract house at the edge
of a line of tawdry floats when one
thought one deserved an open expanse already
fitted with false endings and some swift sniff of the plough still
fragrant among the phrases of camouflaged operas
sung pounding from a tower
prison on the flank of a seriously compromised jubilation—"
Rain on its way in a way disarranged
love by its return deranged
from a sleepover beyond the shackles
of whatever is waking.

THIRTEEN (PYRAMID SCHEME)

Alone in disguise we say the paper cup is full but oh
it might spill over onto the coupons kids have been trading
in uncertain futures belonging
to those who can profit from the surplus of shirts, skirts,
pants, and sandals mating finally in one long
pursuit of the trouble I've seen like a pyramid on a pinnacle
or a string of aliases at this juncture unfree
to remember who made them mark
beautiful value (one for the orange of the oriole) down
out of thin air we were paid to leave
everything behind coming-to without a deal from a dream we find
bogus later, coming-to exactly where we are
but no smarter.

FOURTEEN (COINCIDENCE)

A clock chimes in the athenaeum
between chance and selection unaware
of the complex intricacies of its duet
with sleep and the super-silent reader.
A stand-in would be pining there
leaving you to rendezvous
back at the beginning with just
yourself or some of your seven
brothers in the usual cantilevered
numbers stumped at the size of us
arriving rapid-fire in blather
cramped from the cabin and
bushed from a fit
of citizenship
setting out on a long lazy
road through a puzzling (invented)
subdivision, ruffled above canonical below
in both senses, knuckles
knuckled split on the lip
by chance revealing the microscopical thrumming
of what may be intolerable
but can only be described as inspired
(that the pump in the brain not only works
but chortles) or simply happens
at the same time the silent
slit cuts the coat of the maestro into two
perfect halves and the chime
rings free. "So you think
there will be— ?" "Certainly.
And more so where night pleads out
a harp floats in
on its convention."

FIFTEEN (REVELATION)

"When I went out to get a breath
it was the smoke of manufacture
having havoc slept possessed
conceptless in no more time
than what I needed to begin
green silicate skin an agate face
beating as it were the sun the company
assembled. Those with jug
ears swore, go ahead, take the rock and eat
it up the mind's craving to look
out of a billowing sac clumsy and
critical rules the earth using up
the convention while reveling
in its emptiness. Having taken the advice
to forget absolutely
nothing too literally I met
striving in my bed the slaves
of my less sensitive enemies and freed them—
trees pulled up by greenhorn roots
left to wiggle upside-upward
I'd pierce the stars
with their questionnaires
for little bits of leftover juice
whose cahoots with chance
must be neocortical.
Otherwise we wouldn't search for such evidence."

SIXTEEN (AT THE ZIGGURAT)

So? Autos stream solemn
from unquiet corrals unrestrained.
The knuckle of the world fills up
with sun late and early evening persons
converge on a lot where we
think up tossable wry giants and try
to repress them everything
is filled with dignity nothing
can be contained
in our effort to recapture the stranger part of Sunday
taking the need to be critical
as a lovable foible or foot
buried in loot
stuck in the geometric return of the same
long cartoon ears appearing out of the blue
sandstorm sleep too
is the same everywhere but not the wooden
hills one heads for full of butter
in search of better
ink the eloquent liquid follows from
melody originally slime now mortar
in the aspic of discourse where
the animals are still restless and sing after all
the foundation of heaven and earth
is *actually* on the map! That is the meaning
of this happy hour.

Meanwhile night had begun to fall.

Sources

The sketch, that is a word which awakens in me a great thought. In the violent transports of passion, a man omits the links, begins a phrase without finishing it, lets a word escape him, utters a cry, and falls silent. Nevertheless, I have heard everything. —Diderot

REASON

"Men are mortal," "All the world loves a lover," "Jones believes that Paris is in France," etc.; Willard Van Orman Quine, *Elementary Logic*, rev. ed. (New York, 1965) · "Radio evolves into noise"; Pokémon fantasy · "Got up, felt dubious," "Bought a candle and read *Great Expectations*"; Allen Jaqua, unpublished Civil War diary, 1861-1862 · "Lazy blimps broadcast ..."; Alexei Parschikov, in conversation Helsinki May 2001, proposes an eternal art project in which dreams are screened on the sides of dirigibles.

PROSE OF THE WORLD ORDER

"This alchemical mixing of apparent opposites ecstatically ... ," "dialectical ballast"; Bruce Wilshire, "The Breathtaking Intimacy of the Material World: William James's Last Thoughts," in *The Cambridge Companion to William James*, ed. Ruth Putnam (Cambridge, 1997), 105 · "All I know is what the words know, and the dead things, and that makes a handsome little sum, with a beginning, a middle and an end as in the well-built phrase and the long sonata of the dead"; Samuel Beckett, *Molloy*, in *Three Short Novels by Samuel Beckett* (New York, 1965), 31.

ODE IN PENCIL

"Days raging, as days rage," "star on star," and "the road out of the song" (all paraphrases); Burton Raffel's translation of "A Slate Ode," in *The Complete Poems of Osip Emilevich Mandelstam* (New York, 1973), 134-36 · "A stranger I arrived, / a stranger I depart again ..."; Wilhelm Müller, "Night," unattributed translation from the liner notes for Franz Schubert's song cycle, *Winterreise* (Deutsche Grammophon 447 421-2) · "A stone is nothing but weather"; Mandelstam, from the essay "Talking About Dante," trans. Clarence Brown and Robert Hughes, quoted in Sidney Monas's introduction to *Complete Poems*, 19 · "A ferry is as though departing in the dark toward a saga"; Kevin Davies, "Thunk," *Open Letter* 10, no. 1 (Winter 1998): 75 · "The umpire is fulfilling ancient orders"; William Fitzgerald, *Agonistic Poetry: The Pindaric Mode in Pindar, Horace, Hölderlin, and the English Ode* (Berkeley, 1987), 54.

WHAT THE SAWHORSE SAW

The Sawhorse, a supporting character in L. Frank Baum's *The Marvelous Land of Oz* (Chicago, 1904), is animated by the "Powder of Life," a vial of which is stolen by the boy Tip (who later turns out to be the girl Ozma) from Mombi the witch. Ozma enjoys omniscience in Oz with her "magic picture," which affords her a view of everything, everywhere, all the time. · "(A storm is the sky's only exhalation, as the sky is the storm's only chance of *being*, its sole arena!)"; Marina Tsvetaeva, "Downpour of Light," in *Art in the Light of Conscience*, trans. Angela Livingstone (Cambridge, Mass., 1992), 25 · "Whenever we look up at the sky, we involuntarily have a presentiment; unconsciously we anticipate some sort of 'communication' from there; it seems that 'something' will be addressed directly to me"; Ilya Kabakov, quoted in Boris Groys, David A. Ross, and Iwona Blazwick, *Ilya Kabakov* (London, 1998), 86.

RIOT IN AXIOM

"Men have been talking for a long time on earth, and yet three-quarters of what they say goes unnoticed. *A rose, it is raining, it is fine, man is mortal.* These are paradigms of expression for us"; Maurice Merleau-Ponty, *The Prose of the World*, trans. John O'Neill (Evanston, 1973), 3 · "O then sieze me, dear ones," Hölderlin, "To the Germans in F----- H-----:," in *Selected Poems and Fragments*, trans. Michael Hamburger (Harmondsworth, 1998), 45 · "I will be small among the small, great among the great"; Pindar, "Pythian 3," lines 107-8, in Frank J. Nisetich, *Pindar's Victory Songs* (Baltimore, 1980), 173 · "For I am a little fellow, which is entitled to the great mess by the benevolence of God my father"; Christopher Smart, *Jubilate Agno*, B 45, in *The Poetical Works of Christopher Smart*, 4 vols., ed. Karina Williamson and Marcus Walsh (Oxford, 1980-87).

WHITMAN

"Who goes there! Hankering, gross, mystical, nude?"; Walt Whitman, *Song of Myself* (1855), in *Leaves of Grass* (New York, 1992), 45 (unless otherwise noted, subsequent references to Whitman are identified by page number in this edition). · According to F.O. Matthiessen, *American Renaissance* (London, 1941), 560, Whitman conceived of a national (American) opera including "three or more banjos." · "In vain the plutonic rocks send their old heat against my approach"; Whitman, *Song of Myself* (1855), 57 · "The physical apparatus of the moving image necessitates its existence as primarily a mental phenomenon. The viewer sees only one image at a time in the case of film and, more extreme, only the decay trace of a single moving point of light in video. In either case, the whole does not exist ..., and therefore can only reside in the mind of the person who has seen it, to be revived periodically through his or her memory"; Bill Viola, *Reasons for Knocking at an Empty House: Writings, 1973-1994* (Cambridge, Mass., 1998), 204 · "And this branch pluck'd at random from myself, / It has done its work—I toss it carelessly to fall where it may"; Whitman, "Spontaneous Me," in *Whitman: Selected by Robert Creeley* (Harmondsworth, 1973), 127 · "And I will show that whatever happens to anybody it may / be turn'd to *beautiful* results"; Whitman, *Starting from Paumanok* (1891-92), 183 · " ... and the flambeaus of the night ..."; Whitman, *When Lilacs Last in the Dooryard Bloom'd* (1891-92), 460 · Also from Whitman's *Drum Taps*: "How I could hug them"; "No dainty rhymes or sentimental love verses for you terrible year"; "Saw I your gait and saw I your sinewy limbs clothed in blue"; "trusty rifles"; "hurried and glittering tides,"417, 418, 419, 429 · "I find I incorporate gneiss ... / And am stucco'd with quadrupeds and birds all over," "This minute that comes to me over the past decillions, / There is no better than it and now," "... the other I am ..."; Whitman, *Song of Myself* (1855), 57, 49, 30 · "[W]hat can equal the rich golden flowers of the Cana lutea, which ornament the banks of yon serpentine rivulet, meandering over the meadows; the almost endless varieties of the gay Phlox, that enamel the swelling green banks, associated with the purple Verbena corymbosa, Viola, pearly Gnaphalium, and silvery Perdicium; how fantastical looks the libertine Clitoria.... " (1773-1777); William Bartram, *The Travels of William Bartram* (Athens, Ga., 1998), 98.

ENTHUSIASM

"The scientific outburst that clears the air"–a description of futurist theater by F. T. Marinetti, quoted in Jerome Rothenberg and Pierre Joris, eds., *Poems for the Millennium* (Berkeley, 1995), 1:215 · "Many would agree, ..., that in different dimensions there is different time and it moves in different speeds and different measures. Few have sufficiently considered, however, the infinite speed of the dream-time, the time that turns inside out, the time that flows backward. For ... very long sequences of visible time can, in the dream, be wholly instantaneous—and can flow from future to past, from effects to causes"; Pavel Florensky, *Iconostasis* (1922), trans. Donald Sheehan and Olga Andrejev (Crestwood, N.Y., 1996), 35.

IMAGINATION

"Does the daylight astonish?"; Whitman, "Song of Myself" (1855), 45 · "Reality, unlike the image on the retina or on the television tube, is infinitely resolvable: 'resolution' and 'acuity' are properties only of images"; Viola, *Reasons for Knocking,* 44 · " ... to speak in literature with the perfect rectitude and insouciance of the movements of animals and the unimpeachableness of the sentiment of trees in the woods and grass by the roadside is the flawless triumph of art"; Whitman, preface to *Leaves of Grass* (1855), 13 · "Forced down from the storyteller's promontory, the reader of *Jacques* [*le fataliste*] finds himself a part of, one with, submerged within, the onrushing torrent of consciousness deprived of all access to the consoling visions of a Great Scroll to which he would relate as reader rather than letter"; Thomas M. Kavanagh, "*Jacques le fataliste*: An Encyclopedia of the Novel," in *Diderot: Digression and Dispersion*, ed. Jack Undank and Herbert Josephs (Lexington, Ky., 1984), 157 · "Life ... can never be lived as a 'story,' as an organized, coherent narrative guided by a single, all-encompassing telos"; Kavanagh, "*Jacques le fataliste*," 162.

HAT SCHISM

"For to worship naked in the rain is the bravest thing for the refreshing and purifying [of] the body"; Christopher Smart, *Jubilate Agno* B 224, in *Poetical Works* · " ... gorgeous, indolent, sinking sun ..."; Whitman, "When Lilacs Last in the Dooryard Bloom'd," in *Leaves of Grass*, 462 · "A persistent, if persistently debunked anecdote of the late eighteenth century described Swiss mercenaries in France as perpetually in danger of contracting nostalgia en masse were they to hear [their] native anthem…. French army musicians were forbidden … to play the tune"; Nicholas Dames, "Austen's Nostalgics," *Representations* 73 (Winter 2001): n. 16 · "H.S., Mark, C.S. Barley, H.B., & myself got out on the sly & went out in the country about 4 miles to a husking, had jovial time in company with some colored gentlemen plenty of 'corn juice' & a good supper, two fiddles & any god's quantity of fiddlers, & had a damn good time two of us stayed all night with bro Sims he put us on a feather bed. I slept but little—" entry for 10 December 1861; Jaqua, unpublished diary, 1861-1862 · "The Democratic hands of America have sewed up her own mouth with iron thread"; Theodore Parker, speech of 29 January 1858, cited in Garry Wills, *Lincoln at Gettysburg: The Words that Remade America* (New York, 1992), 118 · "I'll lean back on my adz and gam for a while"; Joshua Slocum, *Sailing Alone Around the World* · "THE MAD TRAGEDIAN HAS COME TO OUR CITY"; news headline announcing the arrival in New York of the actor Junius Brutus Booth (father of John Wilkes Booth), cited in Reynolds, *Walt Whitman's America*, 158 · "As the trees are not dead, though their foliage is gone, so our heroes are not dead, though their forms have fallen"; Rev. T.H. Stockton at Gettysburg, quoted in Wills, *Lincoln at Gettysburg*, 88 · "I was too thoughtful to be happy," "From the dawn of day in the morning, till darkness was complete in the evening, I was kept hard at work in the woods," "I had as well be killed running as die standing," "I remained all night—sleep I did not," "… for I left by daylight," "Thus early I learned that the point from which a thing is viewed is of some importance"; Frederick Douglass, *My Bondage and My Freedom* (New York, 1969), 160, 215, 220, 233, 422.

ROMANTIC FRAGMENTS

"We are still surrounded by mountains of ice, still in imminent danger of being crushed in their conflict," "My spirit will sleep in peace, or if it thinks, it will not surely think thus, Farewell"; Mary Shelley, *Frankenstein; or, The Modern Prometheus* (1818) (New York, 1967), 196, 205 · "Knowing whether an image is true or not, what distance separates the model from the copy, whether the image is an image of death or life, these are among the most fundamental questions posed by the artists of the 20th century"; Didier Semin, "From the *Impossible Life* to the *Exemplary Life*," in Didier Semin, Tamar Garb, Donald Kuspit, *Christian Boltanski*(London, 1997), 63 · "A man touched my arm and said, 'This is not bad, but too late'"; Aharon

Appelfeld, *The Iron Tracks*, trans. Jeffrey M. Green (New York, 1998) · "In the epic, everything has already happened"; Susan Stewart, *Crimes of Writing*, 72.

"My words simply give other people a chance to remember what they already know"; Maurice Merleau-Ponty, *Consciousness and the Acquisition of Language*, trans. Hugh J. Silverman (Evanston, 1973) · "A person is erotically bound to the world. That is a condition of there being a world for him: that is, it is a condition of his sanity"; Jonathan Lear, *Love and Its Place in Nature: A Philosophical Interpretation of Freudian Analysis* (New Haven, 1990), 153 · "A necessary condition of there being a world for this person is that it be a world that is not immediately responsive to his wishes. And so, one might say, it is the essence of the world that it could never be better than good enough"; 157-58 · "Characters exclaim 'yesterday' with nostalgic wonder or uncomprehending fury"; Leo Bersani and Ulysse Dutoit [on *Waiting for Godot*], *Arts of Impoverishment: Beckett, Rothko, Resnais* (Cambridge, Mass., 1993), 31 · "What is essential is not to know whether we are wrong or right—that is quite unimportant. What is important is to discourage the world from concerning itself with us. All the rest is vice"; Beckett, quoting from Céline in his diary, cited in James Knowlson, *Damned to Fame: The Life of Samuel Beckett* (New York, 1996), 217 · "FARM HORN MOB PASTE NOT BE": sample Scrabble play from the 1949 instructions.

"I really think I am nobody. If you work as an artist, you destroy yourself. The more you work, the less you exist; and each time you do an interview a part of yourself disappears. It seems awful, but it can also be a good thing, since it is easier to make art than to live. It's a choice one makes"; Christian Boltanski interviewed by Tamar Garb in *Christian Boltanski*, 8 · "It is as if, in [Stan Douglas's] use of cinema and video, he wants to reveal the structure of an illusion that can no longer be sustained but which is nevertheless deeply embedded in the histories of these media. It is an uncanny apparition of an unmoored subject we used to call 'I'"; Scott Watson, "Against the Habitual," in Scott Watson, Diana Thater, Carol J. Clover, *Stan Douglas* (London, 1998), 66 · "If you live in a country where it always rains you can't expect to fight the rain by organizing a demonstration"; Ilya Kabakov, in Groys, Ross, and Blazwick, *Ilya Kabakov*, 11 · "The order instituted by music is not the primary order of the harmonious society of singers formed by the performance, nor the secondary order that comes into being when the violence of eagle and thunderbolt is suspended; instead the order of music consists in the *articulation* of the ambivalent liquid rippling that is the source of all energy"; Fitzgerald, *Agonistic Poetry*, 146-47 · "If you want me again look for me under your bootsoles"; Whitman, "Song of Myself" (1855), in *Leaves of Grass*, 88 · " ... as when, for instance, having decided to regale myself in a prison cell with stories I shall tell myself"; Richard Wollheim, *The Thread of Life* (Cambridge, Mass., 1984), 69 · " ... as if / The shore were not already more than sufficient"; Horatio, Odes II.18, in *The Essential Horace*, trans. Burton Raffel (San Francisco, 1983), 52 · " ... not in ships or on foot / Will you find the marvelous road / To the games of the people of the North"; Pindar, from *Olympian 3*, in Fitzgerald, *Agonistic Poetry*, 74.

"I constantly fulfill an act of internal sense, which blends with the words and, so to speak, animates them"; Edmund Husserl, quoted in Merleau-Ponty, *Prose of the World*, 31 · " ... and the call to evening roulette in the casino ..."; Mandelstam, letter to Ivanov, August 1909, in *Critical Prose*, 478 · The Artist: "He himself labored happily his whole life, a man unaware that he was on a volcano, while we see his work as flowers on the edge of a precipice"; Merleau-Ponty, *Prose of the World*, 73 · "The plane of the horizontal is desublimatory, associated with 'base materialism'"; Linda Nochlin (quoting Rosalind Krauss) in a discussion of Gericault's paintings of severed heads in *The Body in Pieces* (London, 1994), 21 · Sullivan: as in *Sullivan's Travels*, the 1941 Preston Sturges film. The American landscape painter Thomas Cole (1801-1848) was "pursued by sounds of the axe"; Laurence Goldstein, *Ruins and Empire: The Evolution of a Theme in Augustan and Romantic Literature* (Pittsburgh, 1977), 229 · On the whippoorwill in Tin Pan Alley: Stephen Feld, *Sound and Sentiment* (Philadelphia, 1982) · "It is words that words arouse"; Merleau-Ponty, *Prose of the World*, 115 · "The Hindus of the central provinces of India believe that a twin can save the crops from the ravages of hail and heavy rain if he will only paint his right buttock black and his left buttock some other color, and thus adorned go and stand in the direction of the wind"; Sir James Frazer, *The New Golden Bough*, abridged ed. (New York, 1959), 73 · "Divine obstetrician and embodiment of twilight"; *Rig Veda*, ed. Wendy Doniger O'Flaherty (Harmondsworth, 1981), 78 · "[I]t is a special satisfaction to tell you how much you have enlarged the boundaries of the permissible in the empire of sound." —Debussy to Stravinsky, quoted in *The New Grove Twentieth-Century French Masters* (New York, 1980), 108 · "Apollo hunted Daphne so, / Only that she might laurel grow"; Andrew Marvell, "The Garden," in *Andrew Marvell: The Complete Poems* (Harmondsworth, 1972), 100.

"Very early on in the drawing there is a sense of the passage of time. The ethical or moral questions which are already in our heads seem to rise to the surface as a consequence of this process. Initially I just wanted to draw landscapes, then I realized that the drawings, in themselves, evoked these larger questions"; William Kentridge, interview, in Dan Cameron, Carolyn Christov-Bakargiev, J.M. Coetzee, *William Kentridge* (London, 1999), 19 · On epilepsy: "What strange rain falls on the earth, and what divinity scatters these drops that are men onto the earth, yet makes them fall outside of themselves?" Catherine Clément, *Syncope: The Philosophy of Rapture*, trans. Sally O'Driscoll and Deirdre M. Mahoney (Minneapolis, 1994), 10 · "Friends have eyes and ears, but their flashes of insight are not equal. Some are like ponds that reach only to the mouth or shoulder; others are like ponds that one could bathe in"; *Rig Veda* 10.71, 62 · "At night all cows are black"; Sartre, paraphrasing Hegel's denunciation of Schelling's conception of absolute knowledge, quoted in Clément, *Syncope*, 35 · "It is normally impossible even to look at the places where the inside of the body becomes visible—the twilight of nostrils, ears, mouths, anuses, vaginas, and urethras. The inside is by definition and by nature that which is not seen"; James Elkins, *Pictures of the Body: Pain and Metamorphosis* (Stanford, 1999), 109 · "Everyday life, to Pasternak, is like the earth to a footstep: a moment's restraint and a pulling away"; *Art in the Light of Conscience*, 29. "[Buffalo Bill] Cody was a fool with money. He sunk a bunch of it into something called White Beaver's Laugh Cream, the Great Lung Healer, an herbal remedy which arrived on the market roughly a century too soon"; Larry McMurtry, *Sacagawea's Nickname: Essays on the American West* (New York, 2001), 28 · "Attempting to read the *Jubilate Agno* with a full awareness of its echoes and puns, its miraculous casts into scripture and other texts, induces something like a 'readers sublime,' a state of absolute metaphor in which anything can potentially stand for anything else. Reading *Jubilate Agno* is a process, like Smart's gratitude, with no necessary end"; Clement Hawes, *Mania and Literary Style* (Cambridge, 1996), 169 · "Water, upon which waves, upon which a boat, upon which a woman, upon whom a man. Already thought out in the summer of 1904. Rocking construction" (1906); Paul Klee, *The Diaries of Paul Klee, 1898-1918* (Berkeley, 1964), 206 · "I am a bundle of sensitive particles and everything is touching me and I am touching everything else"; says the character Julie de L'Espinasse in Denis Diderot's *D'Alembert's Dream,* in *Rameau's Nephew and D'Alembert's Dream,* trans. L. W. Tancock (Harmondsworth, 1966), 184 · "It is the most ridiculous structure that I ever made and that is why it is really good"; Eva Hesse (of her construction *Hang-Up,* 1966), in Lucy Lippard, *Eva Hesse* (New York, 1976), 56.

OTIUM

"To a green thought in a green shade," "whetting silver wings"; Marvell, "The Garden" · "Somebody's Somebody"; identification label on a skeleton in a museum work by Fred Wilson, Berkeley Art Museum, spring 2003 · "Tourism and collecting went hand in hand. The satirical poet Eaton Stannard Barrett, noting in 1816 that 'every one now returns from abroad, either Beparised or Bewaterlooed,' claimed to know 'one honest gentleman, who has brought home a real Waterloo thumb, nail and all, which he preserves in a bottle of gin'"; Stuart Semmel, "Reading the Tangible Past: British Tourism, Collecting, and Memory After Waterloo," *Representations* 69 (Winter 2000): 12 · " ... the typically metaphysical expatiation on tears and trees that exude sap," " ... knowledge of the myth only deepens the pertinence," " ... the ... idea is to snatch physical pleasure out of the jaws of death and time; here we are asked to dwell on the obscene appetites of these joint fates"; Friedman, *Marvell's Pastoral Art* (Berkeley, 1970), 110, 111, 117 · "Mr Morgan was enjoying his *otium* in a dignified manner, surveying the evening fog and smoking a cigar"; *OED,* s.v. "otium" · " ... but his hand is stretched out still"; Isaiah 9:21 (King James Version) · "[Richard] Feynman approached the problem *perturbatively*: solutions for complicated interactions could be approximated by adding higher- and higher-order corrections to solutions of less complicated situations; David Kaiser, "Stick-Figure Realism: Conventions, Reification, and the Persistence of Feynman Diagrams, 1948-1964," *Representations* 70 (Spring 2000): 52 · "For they will be in the flaring light or life of the body as the starres in the beams of the Sunne scarce to be seen, unless we withdraw our selves out of the flush vigour of that light, into the profundity of our own souls, as into some deep pit.... Thus being quit of passion, they have upon any occasion a clear though still and quiet representation of every thing in their minds, upon which pure bright sydereall phantasms unprejudiced reason may safely work, and clearly discern what is true or probable"; Henry More, quoted in Friedman, *Marvell's Pastoral Art*, 167 · "... the audience will feel that if the orchestra suddenly stopped pouring forth its influence, the actor would immediately become a statue"; Stephane Mallarmé, "Richard Wagner, Revery of a French Poet," in *Mallarmé, Selected Prose Poems, Essays, and Letters*, trans. Bradford Cook (Baltimore, 1956), 74. · "Everyone sings too much"; Debussy, quoted in *New Grove Twentieth-Century French Masters*.

16 LUCKY DREAMS

"Magnanimous Despair"; Andrew Marvell, "The Definition of Love," line 6, in *Complete Poems* · "I ask, where is the affecting charm my heart finds in this song? ... It is absolutely impossible for me to sing it through without being interrupted by my tears"; Rousseau, quoted in Felicia Miller Frank, *The Mechanical Song* (Stanford, 1995), 20-21 · Johnny Cash, "I've Never Picked Cotton" · Steppenwolf, "Born to Be Wild" · "Mother of God, is this the end of Rico?"; Edward G. Robinson's last line in *Little Caesar*, 1930 · "I really wanted to say many more beautiful things, but I am and shall remain superstitiously opposed to fanfares" (1911); Klee, *Diaries*, 258 · *Borometz*: A mythical animal that grows like a flower on a stalk; Elkins, *Pictures of the Body* · *The Perilous Night*: John Cage's 1945 work · "... agates, for example, begin as green silicate skins lining gas cavities in rocks"; Elkins, *Pictures of the Body*, 41 · "The *Marduk* ziggurat [Tower of Babel] was set within the vast sacred precinct on the southern end of the town of Babylon.... Its Sumerian name was Etemenanki, 'The Foundation of Heaven and Earth'; http://www-lib.haifa.ac.il/www/art/babel.html (map at http://www-lib.haifa.ac.il/www/art/list_Ziggurat.html) · "Color possesses me. I don't have to pursue it. It will possess me always, I know it. That is the meaning of this happy hour: Color and I are one. I am a painter" (1914); Klee, *Diaries*, 297.